Castles

Fiona Macdonald

FRANKLIN WATTS
NEW YORK • LONDON • SYDNEY

First published in 2000 by
Franklin Watts
96 Leonard Street
London
EC2A 4XD

Franklin Watts Australia
14 Mars Road
Lane Cove
NSW 2066

ISBN 0-7496-3703-X

Dewey Decimal
Classification Number: 728.8

A CIP catalogue for this book is
available from the British Library

Printed in Hong Kong/China

Series editor: Anderley Moore
Series designer: John Christopher, WHITE DESIGN
Picture research: Sue Mennell
Illustrators: Peter Bull: 6-7, 22, 24-25
Carolyn Scrace: 10-11, 13, 14, 15, 17, 19, 23, 29

Cover: National Trust Photographic Library/Alisdair Ogilvie
(main picture); English Heritage Photograpic Library (inset)

Interior Pictures:
Illustrations:
Photography: AKG London pp. 5t (Hilbich), 9t, 9m (Jean-
Louis Nou), 14tl and 14tr (Heidelberg Universitatsbibliothek),
16 (Musée Condy, Chantilly), 18t (Heidelberg
Universitatsbibliothek), 25 (Bibliotheque Nationale, Paris)
Arcaid pp. 8 (Alex Bartel), 26b (Mark Fiennes)
Axiom pp. 9b (Steve Jones), 28t (Steve Benbow)
Sylvia Cordaiy p. 28b (Edward O'Neill)
English Heritage Photographic Library pp. 6 (Skyscan
Photolibary), 12, 22, 26t
e.t. Archive pp. 16-17 (Musée Condy, Chantilly), 18b (British
Library)
Mary Evans Picture Library p. 20 (Explorer),
National Trust Photographic Library/Alisdair Ogilvie p. 4-5
Royal Armouries/Leeds, (c) The Board of the Trustees of the
Armouries pp. 3, 21
Skyscan Photolibrary p. 27t
The Stock Market p. 27b

Contents

Castles, forts and earthworks

What is a castle?

Castles are huge, strong houses, where kings and lords once lived with their families, soldiers and servants. They were built to provide safety from attack and to display the owner's rank and riches. Castles were also used as headquarters, from which the owner and his officials could control the surrounding lands. Many castles have been destroyed or have fallen down, but some survive for us to admire today.

➡ Bodiam Castle in East Sussex, south-east England, was built in 1385. It was never attacked, and so survives almost intact.

Castle words

Here are some important castle words. See if you can find them and discover what they mean as you read through this book:

Dungeon	Ramparts
Battlement	Motte
Portcullis	Bailey
Drawbridge	Keep
Curtain wall	Garderobe
Moat	
Machicolations	

Forts and earthworks

Castles, earthworks and forts were designed to protect the people inside from attack. Castles were generally built for a single family and their servants and were occupied in peacetime as well as during wars. But earthworks and forts were usually built for whole communities or an army. They were only occupied when danger threatened.

▶ *Schloss Neuschwanstein, southern Germany, was built in fairytale style for King Ludwig II of Bavaria between 1869 and 1896.*

Fairytale castles

Enchanted castles feature in many fairytales. They can be home to beautiful princesses and have splendid tall towers, glittering golden roofs, jewelled windows and flowers growing all around. Or they can be spooky and scary, crawling with bats and spiders, and haunted by ghosts, ogres and monsters.

Try This!

Draw or paint a picture of your favourite storybook castle, and the people – or creatures – who live there. Is your castle peaceful and welcoming, or scary and dangerous?

European forts and castles

Thousands of years ago, Celtic tribesmen and Roman armies built earthworks and forts in Europe. The first true castles were not built until around AD 900. To begin with, castles were just wooden towers on top of huge mounds of earth, surrounded by a strong wooden fence. Historians call these early castles motte and bailey castles.

▲ This Celtic hillfort in Britain, known as Maiden Castle, is over 2,000 years old. The steep banks of earth sheltered the people inside.

Changing castle design

600 BC – 100 BC
Celtic peoples in Europe build hillforts, cliff-castles and brochs (stone towers used as a refuge from attack).

c AD 100
Romans build forts in conquered lands.

AD 800
Vikings build huge earth-mound fortresses.

AD 850–900
First motte and bailey castles in Europe.

AD 1066–1100
Norman conquerors of Britain build a network of castles, first in wood, then stone.

Norman keep

Most European castles now built of stone, with shell keeps or tall stone towers.

AD 1150–1300
Crusaders introduce Middle Eastern improvements in castle design to Europe, including curtain walls and mural towers (towers built into the walls).

Roman Fort

Crusader-style castle

Motte and bailey

The term motte and bailey castle comes from the Norman French words for mound and enclosed land.
The lord's family lived in the wooden tower on top of the motte, which was called a keep. Servants and soldiers lived in wooden huts in the bailey – the land down below. it was protected by a strong fence.

➡ *A typical motte and bailey castle around* AD *1100. The wooden keep stands on top of the high motte.*

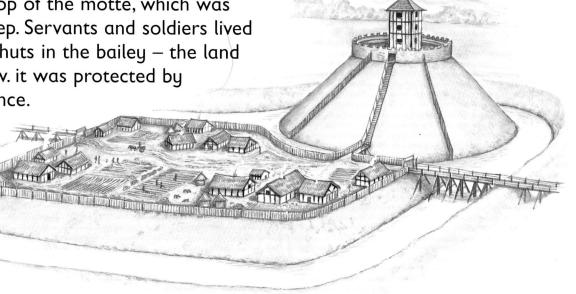

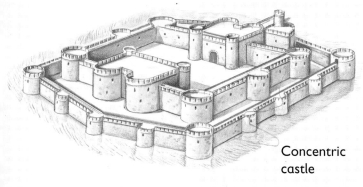

Concentric castle

AD 1270–1350
Concentric castles, the most difficult castles to attack, are built. They have several walls, moats and ramparts, one inside the other.

c AD 1300
King Edward I has many splendid castles built to control the recently conquered country of Wales.

AD 1400–1500
Newly invented cannon smash holes in castle walls. As a result, far fewer castles are built.

AD 1500–1700
Kings and nobles build palaces and elegant country houses instead of castles.

AD 1800s
Mock medieval castles are built in Germany, France and Scotland, after "medieval" style becomes fashionable.

AD 1900s
Castles throughout Europe become popular sites for tourists to visit.

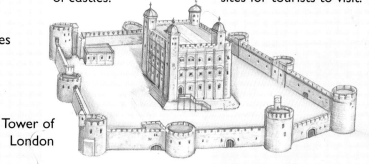

Tower of London

Castles and forts beyond Europe

All over the world, castles have been built to protect communities from attack. Builders in different countries, over the last 4,000 years, invented their own designs for strong forts and castles. These often depended on what building materials could be obtained locally, and on the tools and machines that were available for the workers to use.

Samurai Castles, Japan

The Samurai were landowners and warriors who lived in Japan. From around 1570 to 1690, they built magnificent castles of wood and plaster, each on strong foundations. Samurai castles had wide eaves and graceful curving roofs. Inside, they were decorated with carved woodwork and painted screens. Often, busy towns grew up around the castles.

◀ Hakuro-jo Castle in Japan was built for a Samurai lord around 1600. Its plastered walls are painted brilliant white.

The Kremlin, Russia

The Kremlin fortress in Moscow, Russia, contains a palace, two cathedrals, soldiers' quarters and look-out towers. It was built for the Tsars (emperors) in the 1500s.

◀ *The Kremlin's cathedrals have domed roofs, covered in gold.*

Krak des Chevaliers, Syria

This 'knights' fortress' was built in 1142. At that time, there were many wars in Syria and countries nearby. The wars were known as the Crusades. They were fought between Christian soldiers from Europe and Muslim soldiers from the East.

▶ *Although rebuilt by Europeans, Krak des Chevaliers is still a fine example of eastern defensive building.*

The Red Fort, India

The Red Fort in Old Delhi, India, was built in the 1600s for Shah Jehan, one of the great Mogul emperors who ruled northern India for 300 years. He also built the Taj Mahal in memory of his wife.

◀ *The Red Fort took its name from the colour of the local sandstone with which it was built.*

Castle building and defence

Castles took many years to build. They were designed by a few expert architects and engineers, but built by hundreds of ordinary labourers. Medieval building methods were slow compared with today. Builders had no engine-driven machines to help them, and no electric tools. The wood, stone, earth and rubble used to build castles had to be cut, quarried, moved and shaped by muscle-power.

Did you know...

Stone weighs about 2,000 kg per cubic metre. Its crushing strength (the amount of pressure its weight pushes downwards), is 61,603 kg per square metre.

Stonemasons spread mortar between each layer of stones. The mortar helped spread the crushing load of the upper stones evenly over the ones below, making them less likely to move and the wall less likely to collapse.

Curtain walls

Curtain walls surrounded all the castle buildings like a strong stone shield.

Round towers

It was harder for attackers to make round towers collapse. Unlike square towers, they had no corners, which fell down if holes were dug underneath the foundations.

Machicolations

These were boxes that projected from the walls of the castle and had holes in the floors for dropping stones or boiling oil on attackers.

Defensive features

Castle builders added many defensive features to make their castles difficult to attack.

Gateway defences

The entrance to a castle was always its weakest point. So they were built with thick, iron-studded wooden doors that were hard to break down. Spiked wooden or metal barriers, called portcullises, were even stronger. Drawbridges could be pulled up, preventing access across moats or steep ramparts. Tall gate-towers meant that defenders could shoot down in safety at attackers below.

Ramparts

Ramparts were steep banks of earth or rubble. Attackers had to climb over them to get close to the castle.

Moat

Attackers were easy to shoot while swimming or rowing across moats filled with water.

Battlements

Defenders could hide behind battlements, which consisted of crenels and merlons on top of castle walls, to shoot at attackers below.

Who lived in castles?

Castles were family homes. But they were not like most households today! Hundreds of people lived in a castle, as well as the noble family. They all had jobs to do, keeping the castle running smoothly, caring for the lord and his family, and helping him manage his estates. The average medieval castle household included the lord and his family, his officials and soldiers and servants. There were also farm labourers who lived in cottages on the surrounding land.

The castle household ate together once a day in the Great Hall.

Did you know...

Most castles had no drains. Lavatories – just a wooden seat over a hole cut in a piece of stone – were built inside the thickness of the walls. Waste ran down a sloping tunnel. In the Middle Ages, people often stored their best clothes close to lavatories. They believed the smell kept fleas away. So lavatories became known as garderobes, from the French words *garder,* meaning to look after, and *robes* (clothes).

➤ *A garderobe seen from below. Waste runs out of the square opening into the moat.*

North-east Tower

War-horses and riding-horses lived in the stables.

Castle life

Everything that was necessary for the daily life of a wealthy family in medieval times was enclosed within the walls of the castle.

Try This!

Design a castle that would keep its occupants safe from enemies.

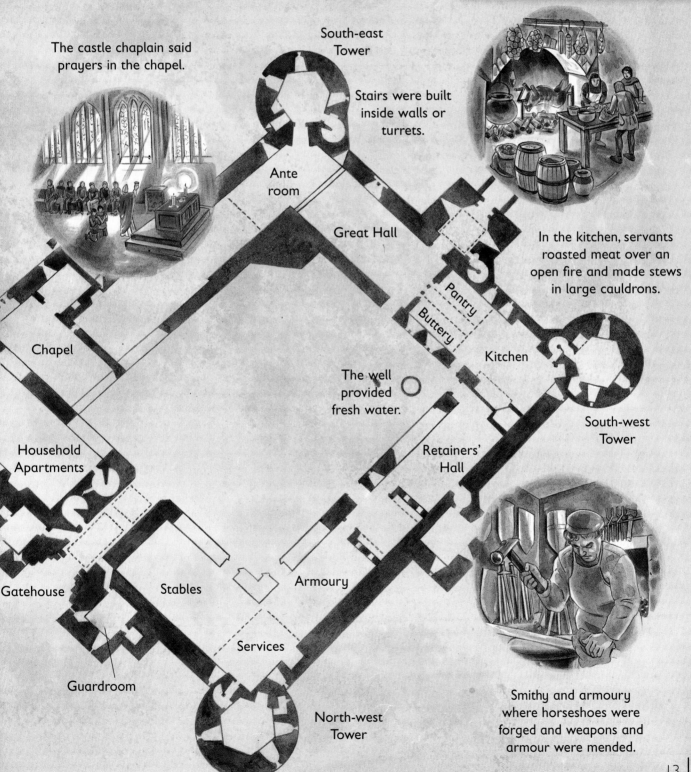

The castle chaplain said prayers in the chapel.

South-east Tower

Stairs were built inside walls or turrets.

Ante room

Great Hall

In the kitchen, servants roasted meat over an open fire and made stews in large cauldrons.

Pantry

Buttery

Chapel

Kitchen

The well provided fresh water.

South-west Tower

Household Apartments

Retainers' Hall

Gatehouse

Stables

Armoury

Services

Guardroom

North-west Tower

Smithy and armoury where horseshoes were forged and weapons and armour were mended.

Castle fashions

Medieval lords and ladies dressed in fine clothes which showed off their rank and riches. Clothes were made of luxury fabrics, such as silk and velvet, and trimmed with gold or silver embroidery, real pearls and fur. Castles were draughty places, so both men and women wore several layers of long, high-necked garments, topped by a heavy fur-lined cloak.

Coronets and kings Make a crown

Imagine you are the lord or lady of the castle and make this stunning coronet.

YOU WILL NEED:

- 50 cm x 60 cm stiff card
- scissors
- gold paint or foil
- sequins or plastic 'gems'
- glue

1 *Measure round your head to calculate the size of your crown.*

2 *Draw your crown on the card and cut it out. Add one or two centimetres on the end for the seam.*

3 *Decorate the card with gold paint or gold foil. Glue on some sequins or plastic gems to look like jewels.*

4 *Overlap the two ends and glue them together. Hey presto! You're noble!*

Castle servants

Women wore long dresses, made of rough linen or wool and covered their head with a kerchief (square of cloth). Men wore thigh-length tunics, long woollen leggings and a hood or cap, also made out of wool. Both men and women wore sturdy leather boots or shoes.

Oranges and cloves Make a pomander

Castles could be very smelly. Moats were polluted by sewage, while manure from the stables added to the stench. To hide castle smells, lords and ladies carried sweet-smelling pomanders (little balls of perfume or spices).

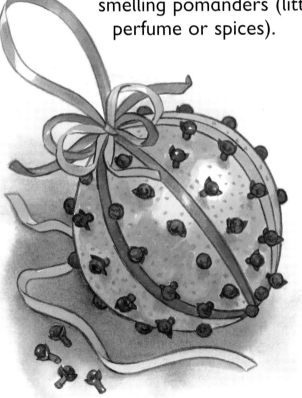

YOU WILL NEED:

- a small, thin-skinned orange – a Clementine is ideal
- 25 g whole cloves
- string
- 1 metre narrow ribbon

1 *Carefully stick the clove-stalks into the orange, perhaps in a pattern. Do not push them in too far or too close together, or the peel will tear.*

2 *Using the string, hang your clove orange in a warm, dry place for at least a week. Do not let it get too hot or damp, or it will rot.*

3 *When the orange has dried enough to stop oozing juices, decorate it with ribbons, and make a ribbon loop to hang it.*

Castle food

In the Middle Ages, ordinary people ate simple food, such as bread, beans, soup and vegetables. Meat, fish, eggs and cheese were luxuries, for special occasions only. The most common drink was ale. Wealthy noble people's food was often highly flavoured with costly herbs, spices, hot pepper, honey, vinegar and wine. Their main drink was wine, often spiced or sweetened.

Castle farms

Food for the people in the castles came from the surrounding land. Many lords' estates were given to them by the king in return for a promise to fight for him in wartime, and help him govern the country. The estate land was farmed by peasants. They either worked for the lord or paid him rent. The lord let them build cottages and work their own small farms, where they grew food to feed their families and to sell. The rent paid by the peasants helped pay for the upkeep of the castle.

◀ *Peasants gather grapes to make wine on land belonging to this castle in Northern France.*

↑ *Servants serve the food as the lord greets his guests. Can you see the pet dogs that have jumped on the table?*

Medieval manners

Medieval people ate with knives, spoons – and their fingers! They did not use forks. Two or four people shared one dish of food. They picked out tasty morsels, then placed these on a trencher (thick slice of bread), before eating.

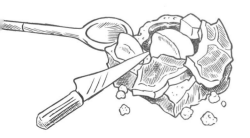

Try This! Poor knights of Windsor

This variation on a medieval dish is a little like the snack we call French Toast today. In the Middle Ages, wealthy knights ate it with wine sauce flavoured with costly spices. This version is cheaper and easier to make.

YOU WILL NEED:

For two people
- 2 slices of slightly stale white or wholemeal bread.
- 125 ml milk
- a knob of butter or 10 ml oil for frying
- 1 egg
- runny honey

YOU CAN TRY THIS!

1 *If the bread crusts are hard, cut them off. Then cut each slice of bread into four equal strips.*

2 *Break the egg into a jug or bowl. Add milk. Beat well together.*

3 *Pour into a big, shallow dish. Dip each strip of bread into the mixture, and let it soak some up. Turn it over or press it lightly to make sure that it is soaked, but don't let it get too soggy.*

4 *While you are dipping the slices of bread, ask an adult to heat a frying pan and put in EITHER the butter OR the oil. Let it get hot, but not brown or smoking. Then ask the adult to fry the strips of bread, a few at a time. Remember to turn them once, until they are golden brown on both sides. Add more oil or butter if needed, until all the strips are cooked.*

5 *Serve your 'poor knights' with honey.*

ASK AN ADULT

Castle entertainments

Music and dancing

During a castle feast, the lord and his guests liked to be entertained by jesters, acrobats, jugglers and contortionists (people who twist their bodies into extraordinary shapes). The most popular forms of entertainment were poetry readings and music. Medieval instruments included fiddles, trumpets, nakers (small drums) and recorders. The lords and ladies also liked to dance.

▲ Many castles had private gardens, where young people of noble birth could meet to enjoy the latest poetry and music.

Minstrel music to play

◆ *This lively tune is a thirteenth-century dance called Dance Royale.*

◆ *Jesters often dressed in brightly coloured clothes and a hat with bells on it to make people laugh.*

Try This! Write a song

One song that would have had a lord's guests spellbound was the legend of the Lorelei. These were young women who lived on the islands in the middle of the River Rhine in Germany. They would sing sweet songs while combing their long, golden hair. Sailors moored safely by the river bank would be lured by the music. They took their boats out into the swirling rapids, only for them to be dashed to pieces on the jagged rocks, while the men drowned in the fast-flowing river.

What kind of song do you think would have this effect? Try to write your own, or compose a simple tune.

YOU CAN TRY THIS!

Knights

Knights were expert fighting men who came from noble families. They were trained from boyhood to handle deadly weapons and heavy war horses. All knights were bound by a code of honour to be loyal to the king or queen.

Some knights owned castles and land. Others served in the private armies of great lords. Being a knight was difficult and dangerous, but it could bring rich rewards of treasure captured in war – and the chance to win fame. The brave deeds of noble knights were praised in minstrels' poems and songs.

◄ Tournaments were dramatic and exciting events. Knights were often injured by a bad fall from horse-back. Lords and ladies looked on from the safety of an enclosed shelter.

Tournaments

In the Middle Ages, mock battles known as tournaments took place. Knights on horseback charged each other armed with blunted lances and padded swords. The winners were the ones who stayed on their horses. Tournaments began as training for war, but soon became a favourite entertainment.

Number work

Chain-mail armour weighed about 15 kg; a suit of plate armour weighed between 20-25 kg.

Find out how much you weigh. Then calculate how much more or less this is than (1) chain-mail armour (2) plate armour.

What does this tell you about how strong medieval knights were?

Long, wooden lance tipped with metal

Metal helmet

Chain-mail body armour

Wood and leather shield

Belt and sword

Surcoat (long tunic) over the chain mail

Chain-mail shoes with spurs

Weapons

Knights fought with a long sword, a dagger, a lance and a mace. Each weapon had a special purpose: lances to spear enemies or knock them off their horses; swords to slash them; daggers to stab at close range; and maces to club them to death.

Knights wore armour for protection. Early armour, known as chain-mail, was made from iron rings linked together. After about 1300, armour was made of shaped pieces of metal fitted together. It was known as plate armour.

◀ *A knight wearing chain-mail armour, from around 1160.*

Prisons and dungeons

Most castles had prisons, where enemy captives and prisoners awaiting trial were locked up. Prisons were often in the strongest part of the castle, so that prisoners could not escape. This was usually the keep, or 'donjon' – later known as the dungeon. Most dungeons were cold, dark, damp and infested with rats and fleas.

⬆ It would be difficult to escape from the high windows in the keep of Rochester Castle, south-east England.

Under lock and key

Often, dungeons were built underground. They were hollowed out of the rock, or built like cellars under the castle keep. Some were shaped like big round bottles so prisoners could not climb out. Others were known as oubliettes. The name comes from the French word for 'forgetting'. Once a prisoner was thrown into an oubliette, he could be forgotten – for ever!

Saved by a song

Richard the Lionheart was king of England from 1189–1199. He was a great warrior who fought in the Crusades in the Holy Land. On his way home through Europe in 1192, he was captured by an old enemy, Leopold of Austria. For a long time, no-one knew where Richard was. According to legend, his faithful minstrel, Blondin, wandered from castle to castle in Austria. At each, he sang a song that he and Richard had written. When he heard Richard singing in reply, he knew he had found his king!

Haunted houses

With so many people coming to a nasty end inside castles, it is hardly surprising that lots of castles are thought to be haunted. There are plenty of tales of spooky castles inhabited by ghosts.

Try This! Finish the poem

Using your own words, write a poem, or a story describing what happened next in the following poem.

Colonel Fazackerley Butterworth-Toast
Bought an old castle complete with a ghost,
But someone or other forgot to declare
To Colonel Fazack that the spectre was there.

On the very first evening while waiting to dine,
The Colonel was taking a fine sherry wine,
When the ghost with a furious flash and a flare,
Shot out of the chimney and shivered, 'Beware!'

From Colonel Fazackerley by CHARLES CAUSLEY

Castles under siege

Castles were difficult to attack. Often, the only way of capturing them was by a long siege. During a siege, attacking armies surrounded a castle and cut it off from the outside world. They also used special weapons called 'siege engines' to try to break through castle walls.

Starved into surrender

People inside a besieged castle were trapped. They fought hard to drive the attackers away, and tried to get messages out of the castle asking friendly armies to come and save them. If they failed, they either starved to death, when their food and water supplies ran out, or else they were forced to surrender.

Siege towers
or belfries let attackers get close to defenders on top of castle walls.

Mangons
worked like catapults to hurl stones at castle defences.

Battering rams

were iron-tipped tree-trunks that smashed holes in stonework and doors.

The end of castles

Metal cannon were introduced to Europe from Asia during the 1300s, completely changing castle warfare. Cannon used the power of exploding gunpowder to fire heavy metal balls which cracked and shattered castle walls. Most castles could not survive a cannon attack. So, after cannon became widely used in the 1400s, few new castles were built.

▲ *A French castle under siege around 1450.*

Trebuchets

were like see-saws. When one end was pulled down, the other flew up, throwing rocks through the air.

Castles today

Castle heritage

The remains of many old castles still stand in countries throughout Europe. They are proud reminders of the bold, ambitious medieval families who owned them, and of the labourers who worked so hard to build them.

Today, castles are favourite places for tourists to visit. As well as exploring the castle building, visitors can also enjoy open-air concerts and firework displays held at many castles. Or they can watch heritage shows, which act out what life might have been like long ago.

▲ Actors in medieval costume fight each other to show visitors what medieval battles were like.

Castle ruins

Many ancient castles have been badly damaged over the years. Their roofs have been torn off by strong winds and rain, and their stone walls have crumbled away. Some castles were abandoned long ago, when their owners moved into more comfortable houses. Some were deliberately wrecked by enemies in war, while others have been destroyed, accidentally, by fire.

◀ Ruined walls and crumbling stone work surrounding the well-preserved Cuellar Castle in Spain.

Preservation and rebuilding

Today, expert craft workers use traditional building skills, such as carpentry and stone-carving, to help preserve ancient castles for future generations to admire. Several castles have been repaired or even re-built, and are now used as museums, hotels or homes for rich and famous people.

▶ Warwick Castle in central England was first built in the 1300s, rebuilt in the 1600s, and is still lived in today.

Modern castles

People seldom build castles today. But soldiers still need strong, safe buildings to shelter in, and to use as a base in wartime. Modern fortresses do not look like castles, but they share some of the same features.

◆ This ___ headquarters in Was___ ___rtress. How many ___

27

What's more...

Sandcastles

For over a hundred years, children and adults have enjoyed building sandcastles on the beach. Today, many sandcastle-making competitions are held in summertime on beaches around the world, and some sculptors even bring sand indoors, to continue building sandcastles all year round.

▶ *This splendid sandcastle was built on the beach in Ibiza, Spain.*

Castle sports

Hunting and and falconry were open-air sports, enjoyed by noble families. The hunters rode on horses, following a pack of dogs which tracked deer and wild boar. Falcons were used to catch small creatures, such as birds and hares. The nobles rode out with trained birds perched on their wrists, then set them free to catch their prey. The dogs and falcons of the castle were cared for by skilled huntsmen.

◀ *Medieval people prized hunting birds like this beautiful peregrine falcon.*

Animal castles

Some animals and insects build homes that look like castles. The most amazing are built by termites and can reach 6 metres tall. These tiny insects live in warm countries and in communities. These are headed by a king and queen, with groups of workers and soldiers who defend the others from attack.

Termites mix chewed-up wood-pulp, from trees and plants, with earth and dung to build their fortresses. Inside, on the lower levels, the queen lays her eggs and the young termites hatch. Higher up, there are store-rooms for plant-pulp gathered by workers, who leave the fortress every day in search of fresh food.

➤ *Entry to the fortress is through a maze of underground tunnels. These are guarded by soldier termites which kill attackers by biting them or spraying them with poison.*

Glossary

bailey: Area of land surrounding (or next to) a castle, protected by a strong wooden fence.

cannon: Big guns that look like long, wide metal tubes. One end of the tube is filled with gunpowder. When this is set on fire, it explodes, shooting a heavy ball of stone or iron out of the other, open, end.

Celtic: Belonging to the Celts, people who lived in Europe almost 3,000 years ago. Celtic civilisation was at its most powerful from around 800 BC to around AD 60.

chain-mail: Armour made of thousands of iron rings linked together. It was usually worn over a wool or leather tunic.

concentric: Describes castles and forts with several walls, moats or ramparts one inside the other.

coronet: A small crown, worn by noble lords and ladies.

crenels: Blocks of stone on top of castle walls or towers. Soldiers could hide behind them to shoot at enemies below.

Crusades: A series of wars fought between AD 1096 and around 1300 between Christian and Muslim soldiers. They both wanted the right to rule the holy city of Jerusalem (in present-day Israel) and the surrounding lands.

earthworks: Huge banks of earth, heaped up like walls around a settlement to keep enemies out.

estates: The lands, fields and farms surrounding a castle that belonged to its owner.

fort: A strong building where soldiers lived and where ordinary people sheltered in wartime.

heritage: Interesting and important things that have survived from the past.

keep: The strong central tower of a castle.

Glossary

mace: A heavy lump of metal or stone attached to a handle by a chain. Used in battles to club enemies to death.

medieval: Used to describe people or things from the Middle Ages.

merlons: The gaps in between crenels at the top of castle walls and towers. Defending soldiers used them for shooting with bows and arrows at enemies below.

Middle Ages: The years from around AD 1000 to 1500. Sometimes also known as 'medieval' times.

moat: A deep, wide ditch, filled with water, that surrounded a castle and helped to protect it from attack.

motte: Huge mound of earth.

Norman French: The language spoken by the Normans – people descended from the Vikings who lived in northern France. They invaded England in 1066.

peasants: Ordinary men and women who lived in little cottages in the countryside and worked on a king's or lord's lands.

plate armour: Protective clothing worn by knights in battle. It was made of carefully shaped pieces of metal, fitted together.

ramparts: Steep banks of earth or rubble that were built around a castle to repel attackers.

siege: A way of attacking a castle by surrounding it with soldiers and stopping food supplies from getting in.

trencher: A thick slice of stale bread, used as a plate. Left-over bits of trenchers were collected after castle feasts, and given to poor people waiting at the castle gate.

Index